Standing on the Outcrop

Poems

Joyce
Compton
Brown

REDHAWK
PUBLICATIONS

Standing on the Outcrop Copyright © 2021 by Joyce Compton Brown

Published by REDHAWK PUBLICATIONS
2550 US Hwy 70 SE
Hickory NC 28602

Robert Canipe, Publisher and Senior Editor
Tim Peeler, Editor
Patty Thompson, Project and Permissions Coordinator

All Rights Reserved

All rights reserved. This book or parts thereof may not be reproduced in any form, stored in any retrieval system, or transmitted in any form by any means—electronic, mechanical, photocopy, recording, or otherwise—without prior written permission of the publisher, except as provided by United States of America copyright law. For permission requests, write to the publisher, at "Attention: Permissions Coordinator," at the address above.

ISBN: 978-1-952485-26-8

Acknowledgements

The author gratefully acknowledges the following publications in which these poems, sometimes in different versions; in one instance an excerpt from a poem, previously appeared. The author also thanks the Appalachian Heritage Festival, Lincoln Memorial University, for the 2nd place award for "Blue Ridge Commons" in the George Scarbrough poetry competition.

Appalachian Heritage "Pine Beetles in a Dry Season"

Broadkill Review "The Clinchfield Sings Siren Songs to the Valley Dwellers, 1910", "Standing on the Outcrop"

Flying South "The Dealer"

Heartwood Literary Magazine "The CSX Circles North Cove at Midnight"

Kakalak "Stroke"

Now and Then "How Workers Learned Their Rights, 1905

Pine Mtn. Sand & Gravel "After Viet Nam"; segment from "Lily Lewis"; "Blue Ridge Commons", "Lula Belle Sings…"

Pinesong; Singing with Jarred Edges "What Pearl Knows[Pearl's Mantra]"

Singing with Jarred Edges "Lula Belle Sings *Amazing Grace*…" (author's chapbook)

Still, the Journal "After the Burning" "Postcards for Pleasure Travelers"

Wild Goose Poetry Review "Broken"

Advance Praise for *Standing on the Outcrop*

"'Standing on the Outcrop' herself, Joyce Compton Brown looks out over the vast peaks and deep valleys and long swoops of land she knows like the back of her hand, it IS her hand, bone and blood---and the voices she hears are her own voices coming from way back....the underside of history, the inside of history. Yet somehow Joyce has the great gift of writing them down and bringing them to us just as they were, just as they are still, peopling those vast and ancient hills. *Standing on the Outcrop* is a treasure.—Lee Smith, author of *On Agate Hill, Dimestore: A Writer's Life,* and *The Last Girls.*

"'Here the stories linger' opens Joyce Brown's lovely collection, a line fulfilled on every page. This book is immersed in place, the shadow of Honeycutt and Linville mountains, the beautiful valley where people till the 'ever cloying earth' or work the mills or own them. They are named and unnamed–Cherokees ousted from their land, Italian railroad workers, Black men and women 'bought or hired,' murdered strikers, shadows in photos or lost under trees and rock. There's joy in language here, whether a tale of loss bluntly told, the lyrical testimony of the laborer released by a stroke to reveal his true nature, or the linguistic dazzle of the Clinchfield railroad singing its siren song– 'and you can/ work shifts /work shifts /work shifts…' You'll remember these people and hear their voices long after you've closed the covers.—Valerie Nieman, author of *Leopard Lady: A Life in Verse.*

"Like a farmer searching for water, in these poems Joyce Brown delves deeper and deeper into her spirit country between Linville and Honeycutt Mountains. Voice, time, and landscape merge, and the essence of the place is revealed, becomes our spirit country too. Brown is one of our state's finest poets."—Ron Rash, author of *Serena* and *One Foot in Eden.*

"Each poem is a masterful piece of a multi-colored quilt like the valley of North Cove in the Fall seen from the precipice above, a vantage point from which to view the stories of people where 'their legends are the landscape of a burnt-off mountain whose trees will rise again.' Brown skillfully sews together stories of beetle blight and wildfires to those of perseverance. She never forgets the forgotten as 'shadows in backgrounds of old photos' or names etched on stone grave markers worn away by time. All the while, a train threads the mountain in and out of tunnels with its grief of coal, soothed by its sound of a 'deep bass note pitched beneath the coyotes tenor note.' With such rich imagery as, 'Burnt trees stand like/ straight black sticks/ as if someone had tried/ to fool around/ for language on the mountain wall/ and failed,' Brown succeeds in telling what the landscape only, prior, held to itself."—Hilda Downer, author of *Bandana Creek* and *Sky Under the Roof: Poems.*

Other books from Redhawk Publications:

All I Wanted by Jake Young

Birdhouse by Clayton Joe Young and Tim Peeler

The Bost-Burrus House by G. Leroy Lail and Richard Eller

Bouquets Hadn't Been Invented Yet by Tony Deal

Food Culture Recipes from the Henry River Mill Village

From Darkness: The Fated Soules Series, Book One by Jan Lindie

Going To Wings by Sandra Worsham

The Hickory Furniture Mart: A Landmark History by G. Leroy Lail and Richard Eller

Hickory: Then & Now by Richard Eller and Tammy Panther

Hickory: Then & Now The Complete Texts by Richard Eller

Hickory: Then & Now The Complete Photograph Collection

Hurdles by Ric Vandett

The Legends of Harper House - The Shuler Era by Richard Eller

More by Shelby Stephenson

Mother Lover Child & Me by Erin Anthony

Newton: Then & Now by Richard Eller and Sylvia Kidd Ray

Piedmont The Jazz Rat Of Cunningham Park by Mike Bruner

A Place Where Trees had Names by Les Brown

Polio, Pitchforks & Perseverance by Richard Eller

Sanctuary Art Journal 2018, 2019, 2020

Secrets I'm Dying to Tell You by Terry Barr

Sittin' In with the Sun by Carter Monroe

Sky Full of Stars and Dreams by Scott Owens

Sleeping Through the Graveyard Shift by Al Maginnes

Suffragettes by Harriett Bannon and Brigette Hadley

Waffle House Blues by Carter Monroe

We Might As Well Eat by Terry Barr

We See What We Want to See: The Henry River Mill Village in Poetry, Photography, and History by Clayton Joe Young and Tim Peeler

What Came to Me—Collected Columns Vol One by Arlene Neal

Win/Win by G. Leroy Lail

Table of Contents

Standing on the Outcrop

Mattie Explains the History of the Cove, 1955

Backwoods Walk

How Workers Learned Their Rights, 1905

Postcards for Pleasure Travelers, 1907

Engines

Photos from the Home Place

The Clinchfield Sings Siren Songs to the Valley Dwellers

Lily Lewis

Recalling the Marion Strike of 1929

The Burial

My Cousin Gives Me a Wall Shelf Made by My Father

Stroke

Auto Tour from the County Seat

Evolution

Malachi

What Pearl Knows

Anticipation

Old Habits

After Vietnam

Broken

Lula Belle Sings

Nelle Speaks with the Wisdom of Experience

Darrell and Evelyn

Blue Ridge Commons

The Dealer

Old Farms

Restless Nights on Linville Mountain

Pine Beetles in a Dry Season

After the Burning

Mountain Swimming Hole in Autumn

The CSX Circles North Cove at Midnight

Small Journey in a Time of Plague

Look Across

Standing on the Outcrop

"As we have misused our richest land, we have misused ourselves; as we have wasted our bountiful water, we have wasted ourselves; as we have diminished the lives of one whole segment of our people, we have diminished ourselves."
Wilma Dykeman

Here the stories linger
nestled in old camp shacks
dissolving into the earth
among rusting shovels and hoes.

They're in a vine-strangled field
of scrub pines and broomstraw
where somebody's garden
once grew in well-hoed rows.

They stick in old yards
where women worked string beans
sitting on shaded front porches,
and men plowed dusty fields.

They're hanging by the roadside
where somebody drove an old Ford
into Coxes Creek after too much shine.
They linger in a caved-in hosiery mill.

They're carried in the air
like spring pollen. All you have
to do is wait, listen in the breeze,
feel the lives come and gone.

Their legends are the landscape
of a burnt-off mountain whose trees
will rise again, whose histories
are twisted pines, clinging in the wind.

Mattie, 1955

Before our families came
    there wasn't much.
They say there were some old forts,
    and arrowheads
the men turned up
    in the plowing.
We made collections,
    sent them to school
        for the kids to show.

They say these pastures
        were good hunting grounds,
And I don't wonder,
        look at this land, these two mountains—
Linville, with its craggy top, Honeycutt
    folding on up toward the highlands,
this river, the clearest water.
        Any living thing would be drawn
            to this valley.

They say the Catawba and Cherokee fought
        over it till we came.
Then they fought us.
        It was perfect for these farms.
You can still see,
        those big old white houses
from before the land got too divided
        and people had to find work.

They say it had a name,
        Conasaga, an Indian word
for *beautiful valley*.
        That may be just talk.
But we use the name
        for our cookbook, and the kids use it
for their school yearbooks.
        They like the way it sounds.

Backwoods Walk

If you hike in the valley
between Honeycutt and Linville
Mountains from the main road
through Gene Brown's field
and on up through Jack Brown's tangled woods
(you should bring a machete
 to fight the cat briars),
you'll come to a few old crooked stones,
some just rocks fetched from the creek,
a few thin small slabs of washed-out granite
with the names eroded into nothing.

A few cockeyed stones hold faint stories
of Italians who were killed
when the railroad was built.
That was just a century ago.
Nobody knows the other names, black men
and women bought or hired to work the big hay fields,
the wheat and corn, to tend the hogs,
take care of all those babies
the farm wives bore in those days.

A few lingered long enough
to become shadows in old family photos.
some stayed and built homes, some perched
on the side of Honeycutt in tarpapered shacks,
climbing down to help the landowners' sons
on that beautiful valley floor, where sometimes
a man shot bullets at their feet just so he could
make them sing and dance.

How Workers Learned their Rights, 1905

In a burial plot
designated for slaves
and descendants
in the woods
on Honeycutt Mountain
below the railroad tracks
built by Italian immigrants
shipped to New York
down to the Carolina Mountains
to blast and dig the tracks
to carry coal
out of Virginia
to the coast,
five unnamed men lie buried,
lost to their descendants.
They mustered strength
to demand payment
for their work.

Locals were deputized,
the mining camp was stormed,
bodies were buried.
Everyone went back to work.

Postcards for Pleasure Travelers, 1907
Altapass Foundation Reprints

I

"The long veranda caught the breeze and
provided shade that treated these wealthy visitors…"

Ladies basked on scenic porch
and rocked their cares away
in frilly damasked gowns
while men admired the view
in tailored linen shirts
while coffee was served to all
above the ruts of rock
while underneath the cliffs
heat-dripped workers built the roads
to ease their leisured paths.

II

"Eastern European immigrants
   who rarely got along with each other…"

They came to
build the tracks
to carry rich men's coal
down the mountain's face
left snaggle-toothed with mines
grim with blackened hate
for wages never paid
for bodies tossed aside
and folded under gneiss.

III
"Italian Workers played badminton"

Did the 'Tally boys' enjoy
swinging feather tuffs
under overseer's care
in a makeshift world
where dawn was filled
with pick-axe rings
and tunnel blasts
and rocks rolling over
damaged corpses of friends?

IV
"Leisure seekers and journalists were
awed by the mountains and the construction
of the loops."

Were they awed
by the bodies
buried beneath the rocks?
Dark eyed young men
fled from barren peaks
in Italy to dreams
of work and plenty
in a green-capped land?

Engines

After the railroad came
the locals watched for fires,
those big black steam engines
a force to be obeyed.
Pulling those coal cars
might set off a spark
on the mountainside.
The men would come
together, crawl
all over Honeycutt and Linville,
catching fires before they
got out of control,
especially in a dry season.
Later, the trains were sleek.
Their engines quiet green,
easier on the men who kept them.
But those who remembered
missed the black boiling hiss
of the old steamers
who always reminded them
of some angry God
they were pleased
to serve.

Photos from the Homeplace

Do we speak of the shadows
in the backgrounds of old photos,
darkened figures of servitude,
their stories untold.

A few jokes cling
to memories of darker faces
some undefined guilt
carried by newer generations.

And then, there's the understanding
between the flat land and the hollers,
the pioneers on the green valley floor,
those who served them tucked up in corners.

That code collapsing
as the land shrank, the factories
came. They came from valley
and holler, breathed in the same fumes.

The Clinchfield Sings Siren Songs To the Mountain Dwellers, 1910

While
they
were
sleeping
in their
cold, hard
rooms,
the train
thundered,
shook
them
away
from
fields,
hoes,
their mules,
bellowed.
come on
come on
come on
we'll give you
money
a house
a church
and you can
work shifts
work shifts
work shifts
and then
go to bed
go to Bed
go to Bed
rest easy
easy easy
down in
Marion
town.

Lily Lewis

I went to the field and ploughed.
Lily Lewis Price

Lily came from Halltown up in the corner of the county, saved and baptized in the creek that flowed right by her house before they damned it up to make Lake James and drowned old Halltown right off the map, so all that's left is brambles, hunting land, and a run-down graveyard. But she'd moved her mother to town by then, got herself a little shack and a job in the cardroom, made enough to feed her mama, keep them from starvation. Twelve-hour shifts— even so it was easier than she'd lived since her daddy died, when she was ten, when she and her mama'd ploughed and planted to grub a living for the little ones left behind.

The women done as much as the men,
if not more. They always do in everything.

Lily didn't rush to marriage. She'd seen how men could fail. She'd worked since she was ten to stay alive, keep her mama going. Jack Morris seemed right kind, helped her tend the neighbor whose skin was seared at work. But when the baby came, Jack drifted on, came back a while, then faded on to those dark shadows found by men who can't abide the harshness of the light. In the mill, the bosses waited: twelve hour shifts, production piece pay, the grinding ringing noise that left her deaf in her old age.

Mr. Baldwin had made a speech
telling us about how good we had
everything.

Lily tired of lower pay and stretching shifts. When the switch was pulled to urge the strike she walked right out. But Baldwin fired her, cut her loose. Nothing left to do but watch the coffins of six dead union men as they drew down Main held up by their friends. Not a local man of God gave voice to speed them on their journey home.

There was all those caskets there
and I can still see them in my
memory.

When they heard her voice at those meetings in New York, that one small mountain voice
which spoke of stench and blood, the listeners pledged their help. The power of her words made clear the striker's fate, brought money to buy food. Lily would go home
to live her goodwife life. But she'd done something right, she knew. She'd do it all again.

Recalling the Marion Strike of 1929

"The women were the worst,"
Mac said, his old voice
quivering in bitter memory.
"They'd call you scab, yell
'Suey suey suey' in your face!
Aunt Sally tried," cried Mac,
tears ponding round his eyes.
"She kept the factory going
when the place was overrun
with too much cloth, and
them wanting more pay.
Nothing to do but close."

They never stopped—marched,
cooked the shabby meals, took
turns tending babies,
propped up plyboard homes
when the mill owner kicked
them out with their cook stoves
and cornshuck mattresses.
Nothing to do but fight
for those kids in shanties
sating their gnawing guts
with fatback and mush.

The Burial (Oct. 1929)

Six workers of the textile mill
In cold blood were shot down.

>*Welling and McGhee*
>*'The Marion Massacre,' 1930*

After the coffins were carried
down the street, and Sherriff
Adkins was declared not guilty,
everybody went home to forget,
or left the county, or the state.
Let Welling and McGhee
lay the story down on a 78 in
West Virginia—hide their names.
It's ever the same old story
For the laborers of our land
They're ruled by mighty powers
And the riches they command.

They were from mining country,
knew about bosses and men
worked to the bone. Later
the careless superior scholars
sneered scholarly insights—
too vaudeville. Too preachy,
a footnote to be buried,
an old song to a rusty tune,
outdated, like the dead men
whose names are carved
on a square stone
behind a chain link fence
where blood rots in the ground.

My Cousin Gives me a Wall Shelf Made by My Father

My father was a thin man
whose lips held a drooping cigarette
as he toiled at Johnson's furniture factory
in the vapor laden air.

After work he'd pick up scraps
good for tinkering, building small gifts
with his restless hands.
He liked cutting and trimming,
inlays and dark stains, sometimes paint.
He'd make little stools and corner shelves,
tiny chests, and sometimes repairs,
a factory man who'd rather work a shift
than bend and toil on ever cloying earth.

They say he loved string music,
driving up the mountain with his friends,
drinking with the boys for a while.
He chose to join that tribe of lonely men
who drove to work, breathed the fumes,
smoked the cigs, tinkered with the by-products
of their solitary lives to keep themselves distant
from fireside and tight hearth.
When they died, they left haphazard
pieces for their wives to pick up,
stories floating in old closets
for daughters to breathe in
like incense as a way of knowing.

Stroke

Afterwards he was free
to speak a new language,
come back to tell them all.

They strained to understand
to interpret his assertions
to feel his newfound power.

He told them how
he'd hated factory saws
the whine of lathe and blade.

Told them how
the smoldering glow
held by tight-closed lips

kept him from
trying to tell
what they didn't

want to hear.
How he'd loved
his fingers shuffling

guitar strings
that flatpick style
speaking its own sad voice

milking the cow
in his own sweet barn
before everybody else was up

They couldn't see
the fiery tongue
above his head.

They couldn't feel
the pyretic fury
in his mind.

But now he was
at center, felt the
glow from lips of fire,

felt the heat
in seething brain.
felt the gift

of flaming tongue,
watched them all
leaning inward.

Auto Tour from the County Seat

Drive by old factories and mills
where people worked and lived,
the defunct furniture plant,
the memorial cotton mill sign.
Come back through Main Street,
and stop at the local crafts shop.
Maybe try Bruce's Fabulous Foods.
Then head north toward farmhouses
still white on the valley floor.
Turn up a creekside road—
Honeycutt, Coxes, or Stillhouse.
Cross the tracks to their old places
which they left daily to get to work.
Get out and walk a weedy field,
a cemetery beside a white church.
Stop at a *No Trespassing* sign
nailed to the power pole at a trailer
hooked up to a TV dish. Turn around
by the orange tractor parked in the shed.
Detour through Pitt Station Road,
its name from steam engine days.
They came from this valley to town jobs,
or never really left— or came back home.
Before you turn around, breathe
in the landscape they love
beyond reason or wealth.

Evolution

After the factories
came and went,
the land held on
in fields and pastures,
old homes still white
in that mountain light
like some Hallmark card
among cedars and pines,
surrounded by the blue-white
of snow, the lights of the past
on valley floor, the others
tucked away in the hollows
and folds, in shacks
and trailers, across the tracks,
deep rooted still.

Malachi

There is a darkness
within the greenest of valleys,
sometimes hidden in the
outlying hollows, where men
tried to make a living with corn,
sometimes hidden
within the mired heart
of whiteness.

A man tortured a black child
who lived within a young man's body,
called him and his all the ugly words
born out of ignorance and despair.
When the poor child fell victim
to suggestion, and killed his tormenter,
they sent him to a white man's prison,
then let him loose after too many years
so that he died a victim of white lightning,
carelessness, the pale fog of indifference
reaching into the Blue Ridge Mountain coves
deep within the pastures of heaven.

What Pearl Knows

Pearl McCall Bates,
1906-2008

The corn will be coming in soon.
You need to come get you some.
It'll be coming in the last of the month.

That bear was eating out of the dog's bowl
here a couple weeks ago.
He just looked at me
and kept on eating.
I thought about telling Virgil
to come over here and shoot it
but he wadn't doing any harm.
Everthing needs to eat.

They was a little turtle
eat out of it yesterday.
I just let it alone.

Anticipation

Virgil
keeps two
photos in
his trailer
one his wife,
the other
his girlfriend.
He swaps them
out if he knows
they're coming
and if he doesn't
he just won't
let them in
till he has
the right
woman
upright
and dusted.

Old Habits

Pearl gets up
at four
to fix Virgil's
breakfast because
she's always
been up at four
fixing somebody's
breakfast and she's
used to it. Virgil
gets up to eat it
cause he can't
half sleep since
Vietnam took
his health and
his uncle's shine
took what was
left.

After Vietnam

The VA paid for
Virgil's special shoes
to soothe his battle-
warped feet which
could not bear the weight
of a straight path back
to the mountain life
he'd planned but
left him stranded
in his old blue Chevy
on a railroad crossing—
motor humming
body slumped
head lolling
in oblivion
to all the trains
coming and going,
too weary
to give a damn.

Broken

Pearl cried at the sight of us.
"I thought you was mad at me"
as if we could be angry at a battered
soul, ninety-nine, finally downed
with a broken hip, finally driven
to dutiful daughter's bed,
homesick for a hill two miles away.
"It's the prettiest place.
If Arville hadn't dragged
them old camp shacks
down there for our house.
If we'd just a had a nice
house on it. But we didn't
starve. We always ate good
and we always shared with
everbody." Margie asks if we
could use a few cucumbers
and a head of cabbage. We
could. She goes out to the garden
to cut the freshest for us,
her own kitchen laden with harvest.

"We always shared," Pearl says,
and she cries on my shoulder.
"The roof started leaking
where them two camp houses
was put together. And we paid
the man five hundred dollars
to fix it. But where he walked
he musta broke in the roof
so we had to move my bed
into the other side with the table
and the living room. And there ain't
hardly any room to move around
with everthing on one side
and still I'd rather be up there

right this minute than sitting here
in Margie's house. And I don't
reckon I'll ever get to go back
home." And she cries on my
shoulder. Little Pearl, her legs
wrapped in white, her eyes
shut tight against the light
of a well windowed house.
Her own dark shelter
shines bright in her heart.

Lulu Belle Sings at the Franklin Reunion

Lulu Belle sings "Amazing Grace"
Without Scotty's harmony to soften the sound
And without his rhythm guitar to hold it steady

So she sings slow and loud with jarred edges
Like rusty cast iron without the oil of kitchen comfort
Like strong rusted bells out in the pasture
Singing and singing to the bending grass.

Nelle Speaks the Wisdom of Experience

In her youth she'd got by with one—
one coat, one Sunday dress,
one pair of shoes, one restless daddy
who wouldn't keep a job.
They'd had one car, always
breaking down. Her Gene
hadn't held up as she'd wished.

Now she was eighty and alone.
She'd got herself six mowers
and a regular mower repair man.
"Just in case," she said.
"You never know when one
will stop working. You can
always use a spare."

Darrell and Evelyn

are living the hard life
in their doublewide with its
built on screen porch
where they keep the dogs.
With Evelyn's failing heart
and Darrell's surging sugar,
they are on the downside
of life's hopes and dreams.

Still, they drive up Peppers Creek,
go to afternoon singings
though Evelyn's voice is weak.
Darrell rides his Kubota
down to Stillhouse Creek
where he's blasted the pasture
into a muddy rock quarry.

Sometimes he hauls off a load
to sell to the local rock business,
and he still trades guns
with the Yankee retirees
who live over by the golf course.
They bring their fine cars
out here right to his door
and he'll come out to make a deal.

Every day, Darrell practices
his marksmanship
on his own shooting range
right beside his trailer
so everybody can hear,
just in case.

Blue Ridge Commons

> *"For them, the woods are richly historical. ... They go out with fathers and uncles and cousins and so on. They go to places that their ancestors have gone to for a century or more. They're inheriting this sense of history"*—Kathryn Newfont

Darrell scraped a road
right through our land,
hauled off boulders
we'd placed to slow the
flood down mountainside—
drove his Kubota
through our pine saplings,
tore out our campfire ring
to get up the mountain road
where he'd always gone
unfettered, where his
daddy had gone before.

He didn't know the term—
Blue Ridge Commons—
But our grandfathers
had worked a still together,
had named the creek
Stillhouse. Our fathers
had shared a little shine.
Darrell had learned to swim
in the creek's cold depth.
He'd hunted in those woods.
His uncle grew a little pot
down there behind the barn.
His kids had found crawdads,
learned about water snakes,
timber rattlers, bear season.

He had his special chair
for practicing his shooting
under the giant poplar tree,
by our *No Trespassing* sign.
He'd fire, the empty shells
spilling out to the ground,
under the green carpet
of May-apple leaves.
This land was free for the using,
the deed written only in the heart.

The Dealer

Howard's palsied hands
jitterbug across yellowed plats
as he speaks of deeds,
ancient borders, deals he's
made for family lands.

His rusted-out Ford pickup,
groaning its half a million miles,
bucks up the gully-washed
red road of Pearlie's old place
throwing papers and caps,
cups and plastic junk
off the dashboard.

He'll trade this place
for our family field,
he says, wash-worn
overalls hanging
on his lanky bones
as he lights up,
coughs, takes a draw.

He'd scrambled up to grown
in one of those little hollows
left vacant by prosperous
farmers on the valley floor.
Now he collects trailer lots
flatland farms and old home
places, shuffles them all
like fifty-two pickup,
one more deal before
the last cough, the last
shaky hold before the fold.

Old Farms

They tried to hold to home,
these old fathers whose fathers
had cleared the land, made pastures and fields,
built barns, churches, wide-porched homes for shade.

They tried to keep the land,
its rolling fields of grass,
its streams their fathers had loved,
sweet hay in the autumn light.

The wives and daughters helped,
drove to work, came home to garden chores.
If only one son will stay, if only one daughter
will marry a local boy, the house will stand.

Restless Nights On Linville Mountain

Coyotes have
claimed the mountain
as their own—
stalking and singing,
running in packs
searching for
that which is
most vulnerable.
The only sound
that swallows their
howling echos
is the whining
of the coal trains
passing through,
carrying chunks
of West Virgina,
moving closer
to the coast.

Pine Beetles in a Dry Season

Winter's wrung wrong side out
on Linville Mountain.
Poplars and maples glow green in crevices.
Scrub pines stand brown and dying on roils.
Their limbs drip grey snow on galax at their feet.
Death oozes out pores of bark, sticks to the touch,
waits for the last green needle.

Scrub pines are waste trees,
fit for pulp mills, squirrel nests, bear claws.
Shallow rooted knuckles cling for years
to Linville's thin soil, slide into rock slams, clutch
till winter wind rips out their hearts,
till ice pulls them headlong toward the soil
where cones have thrown light seeds to start again,
where they rot to mulch more pine.

But now they're eaten from within,
shelter for their own destruction,
winter death in summer drought.
In a dry year even the chip
and shred of pulp mills
can't keep up with beetle jaws.

After the Burning

The fire, reported March 16, is burning near Shortoff Mountain in the Grandfather Ranger District of the Pisgah National Forest. A U.S. Forest Service spokesman said investigators believe the fire started from lightning during the first week of March.

Linville Mountain sits
stark with pale bone face,
shaping its own monument
of quartzite grey
shining like death
in the sunlight
against the valley floor.
Burnt trees stand like
straight black sticks
as if someone had tried
to fool around
for language on the
mountain wall,
and failed.

Mountain Swimming Hole in Autumn

All is poised for descent, leaves
brown-veined with age, some curled
crisp, some floating flat on the membrane
of water's surface, some already sunken,
dissolving within the still waters.
The water is placid about it all.
The rotting log piercing its depth.
Leaves--sycamore, maple, oak—
jaundiced, leathered, webbed,
spindly limbs, twigs, one season's
growth, one overarching limb
bent earthward in resignation.

The distant bank won't give focus,
unidentifiable browns and grays—
perhaps a shadow person, blue shirt
reflected, a flash of living pink within
the decaying debris. Waiting for what?
Perhaps only an accidental refraction,
the dead and decaying waiting
for the boys who played there
when life was warmer, when leaves
were green and limbs were straight,
when the diving in was easy
and the crawling out was sure.

The CSX Circles North Cove at Midnight

It rumbles in the dark
like a deep bass note
pitched beneath coyote's
tenor yelp, as it has
for a hundred years,
from West Virginia coal mines
through the valley. It snakes
down Linville Mountain
toward factories long dead,
past depots boarded up,
converted to tourist sites.

It passes smoke stacked plants
where mysteries are made,
where trucks wait
to carry the load.
It slides on down to
Piedmont towns where
empty buildings loom
rust-red in the night.
Dead cotton mills
and furniture plants squat
near boarded company stores.
It rolls down to the flatlands
to a few coal plants
still churning power
before the final shutdown,
moves on down to port towns
hauling oil in tank cars
for big ships to carry
on to foreign ports.

At journey's end cargo cars sit
in great tracked lots, waiting,
where kids write their songs
of *I am here* with spray paints
and bold words, indecipherable
to men rambling by, in language
no clearer than the coyote's yap,
ignored as commonplace,
the jibberings of the young,
irrelevant to the journey

Small Journey in a Time of Plague

There is something peaceable
about the mountains,
something silent and distant
from the messiness
of humankind—This valley
is a quiet deep space
between the forces,
Honeycutt and Linville,
defining the land.
We come for the blue aura
of quietude. We come to walk
the land, because the air is clear
and meadow-scented,
and the place is ours
for this life anyway.

We come where boyhood
once shone sunny and easy.
The house has burned away,
but here is the old lawn,
the field, saplings and underbrush.
It is good to pull pine sprouts,
to cut away bramble, to choose
which too-close tree
should be sacrificed
for the other to thrive.

Here where the warm air
and bright sun fill the morning,
we hear only highway humming
passing through the valley,
a few birds above. We can walk
a ways up Honeycutt Mountain,
behind Tommy's place
into the woods.
It's a Coronavirus day,
and we are wading through a slush

of autumn leaves among the pine
saplings, their green fans brushing
 our skin, letting us pass.

We wander into an old cemetery
barely able to tell its own story.
Trees grow up through sunken graves,
shoving rock headstones—
leaves in abundance fill the plots,
sunken and oblong.
All those stories lie there deep
under leaves adorned by fallen
pinecones. Beneath it all
are those whose grandchildren
would not know where to find them
in this thick woods with no path.
Maybe we'll talk with Tommy
about those old graves.

We walk up to the Ashford cut,
look deep into the crevasse
as the train tears through,
the clacking and warning unstoppable,
curling like a patterned snake,
white coiled within the pass,
moving through the mountain,
its head small and distant,
while here within the ravine
it still rattles and screams.
It's a mystery in this valley—
what is coming and going,
and why.

When we come down we hear
that Tommy has fought and lost.
The forces were relentless
and without mercy across the land,
but Tommy's death proclaims
it real, gives it a name for all
the valley to hear. Tommy's little

buildings, set in the greenness
of his pristine fields, shudder his loss,
here where the grass obeyed
his vigilant command.
The mountain earth
sighs, shifts, resets itself
for a new age.

Looking across

the fog shuffles
     within
         the folded mountain

whispers
     old stories
        of before we were

Notes

"Blue Ridge Commons." Kathryn Nufont published *Blue Ridge Commons: Environmental Activism and Forest History in Western North Carolina* (2012, UGA Press) in her discussion of the "Commons" as "access to forest historically regarded as semi-public" to those who live in regional and cultural communities nearby.

"Lily Lewis." Lily Lewis was a textile mill worker and activist involved in the infamous textile mill strike of 1929 at Marion Manufacturing Company in McDowell County, NC, which resulted in the sheriff and eleven deputized individuals killing six unarmed strikers on October 2, 1929.

"Lula Belle Sings." Lula Belle and Scotty, a singing duo, were fixtures on the original Grand Old Oprey until they retired in Spruce Pine, NC, where Scotty later died.

"Recalling the Marion Strike of 1929." "Mac" is a pseudonym for a works supervisor at Marion Manufacturing Company during the strike. He remained loyal to the owners, the Baldwin family from Baltimore, MD, particularly to a member of the family known as "Aunt Sally."

About the Author

Joyce Compton Brown is a Pushcart nominee and author of two chapbooks, *Bequest* (Finishing Line) and *Singing with Jarred Edges* (Main St. Rag). She attended Appalachian State University where she met and married Les Brown, whose Blue Ridge origins sealed her love of Appalachian landscape, culture, literature, and especially roots music. She received her doctorate at the University of Southern Mississippi and taught at Gardner Webb University, with occasional summer forays into workshops in poetry and Appalachian studies. Nature, her small town family childhood, and music inform her poetry. She also enjoys dabbling in art and creative non-fiction.

www.ingramcontent.com/pod-product-compliance
Lightning Source LLC
Chambersburg PA
CBHW031217090426
42736CB00009B/958